13 JULY 1961

๒

A LIST OF HIS

PUBLISHED WRITINGS

PRESENTED TO

JOHN DOVER WILSON

ON HIS

EIGHTIETH

BIRTHDAY

๒

CAMBRIDGE

AT THE UNIVERSITY PRESS

1961

CAMBRIDGE UNIVERSITY PRESS
Cambridge, New York, Melbourne, Madrid, Cape Town,
Singapore, São Paulo, Delhi, Mexico City

Cambridge University Press
The Edinburgh Building, Cambridge CB2 8RU, UK

Published in the United States of America by Cambridge University Press, New York

www.cambridge.org
Information on this title: www.cambridge.org/9781107621817

© Cambridge University Press 1961

First published 1961
Re-issued 2013

A catalogue record for this publication is available from the British Library

ISBN 978-1-107-62181-7 Paperback

J. Dover Wilson

JOHN DOVER WILSON

English Lector in the University of Helsingfors, Finland, 1906–1909

*Lecturer in English at Goldsmiths' College, University
of London, 1909–1912*

*H.M. Inspector of Adult Education and Continuation Schools under
the Board of Education, 1912–1924*

*Professor of Education in the University of London,
King's College, 1924–1935*

*Regius Professor of Rhetoric and English Literature
in the University of Edinburgh, 1935–1945*

Trustee of Shakespeare's Birthplace, 1931; Life Trustee, 1951

Fellow of the British Academy, 1931

Honorary Fellow of Gonville and Caius College, Cambridge, 1936

Companion of Honour, 1936

Honorary Member of the Deutsche Shakespeare-Gesellschaft, 1939

*Trustee of the National Library of Scotland, 1946;
vice-chairman, 1951–56*

Honorary LL.D., University of Natal, 1949

Honorary D.Litt., University of Durham, 1950

Honorary LL.D., University of Edinburgh, 1950

D. ès L. hon., University of Lille, 1953

Honorary D.Lit., University of Leicester, 1959

Honorary D.Lit., University of London, 1960

CONTENTS

ABBREVIATIONS

CHEL   *Cambridge History of English Literature*
MLR   *Modern Language Review*
RES   *Review of English Studies*
TLS   *The Times Literary Supplement*

5

PREFACE

When two of Professor Dover Wilson's friends began to compile this bibliography, they soon recognized the need to consult him in order to ensure against oversight. He has not only drawn attention to many items in the following list, but has contributed several characteristic comments. The arrangement by sections and the titles of the sections are also his. Within each section arrangement is by the year of publication, and within each year by chronological order, in so far as that can now be readily established, except that books of which Professor Dover Wilson is the author or the editor are placed first in each year.

I

ANONYMOUS ARTICLES ON
FINLAND AND RUSSIA

1 Articles written as Special Correspondent for the *Manchester Guardian*. [The most important was the earliest and fullest account of the 'execution' of Father Gapon early in 1906 by the Social Revolutionaries under the instruction of Rutenberg, who afterwards became one of the founders of Israel—an account which was confirmed six weeks later in all detail by a brochure issued from the Social Revolutionary Executive Committee sitting in Paris. These details were supplied, however, the day after the 'execution' by Konni Zilliacus, father of the Labour Party politician, who had himself got them from Rutenberg, flying from Russia through Finland.]

1906

2 'The Aims and Methods of the Social Revolutionary Party in Russia.' *The Independent Review*, XI, 137–50, under the pseudonym Wildover Johnson.

1914–15

3 'Russia and her Ideals.' *The Round Table*, V, 103–35.

II

CONCERNING EDUCATION

1921

4 HUMANISM IN THE CONTINUATION
SCHOOL. Board of Education. Educational Pam-
phlets, no. 43. [An elaborate pamphlet written in
preparation for the opening of compulsory part-time day
continuation schools for all adolescents of 14 to 18, as
prescribed in the Act of 1918, though owing to the
'Geddes Axe' never brought into being.]

5 *The Teaching of English in England.* Being the report of
the departmental committee appointed...to inquire into
the position of English in the educational system of
England. [The committee sat from May 1919 until 1921.
JDW wrote chapter v, 'English in Commercial and
Industrial Life'; in chapter viii ('Literature and Adult
Education'), sections 232–8, 'Literature and the Nation',
249–52, 'Literature in Workers' Educational Association
Classes'; and in chapter ix ('Some Particular Aspects of
the Teaching of English'), sections 254–66, 'The Problem
of Grammar'.]

1927

6 *The Mind.* By Various Authors. A series of lectures
delivered in King's College, London, during the Lent
Term, 1927. Edited by R. J. S. McDowall. [The object
of the course was to present 'a general idea of the mind
as viewed from several academic standpoints'. JDW
contributed a lecture on 'Education', i.e. 'the mind con-
sidered from the point of view of the study of education'.]

1928

7 THE SCHOOLS OF ENGLAND: A STUDY IN RENAISSANCE. Based on a series of lectures first delivered in King's College, London. Edited by JDW. London: Sidgwick & Jackson, Ltd. [Besides an editorial note, JDW contributed 'The Schools and the Nation'.]

8 'Adult Education in Yorkshire.' *The Journal of Adult Education*, III, no. 1, October 1928. [This journal was founded by JDW, and edited by him from 1926 to 1928. For his account of its genesis, see *Adult Education*, 1952.]

1929

9 'Adult Education in England.' *The Nineteenth Century and After*, CVI, 346–55.

1931

10 (14 February.) Review of *Harrow Lectures on Education*, ed. J. Coade, and of L. P. Jacks's *The Education of the Whole Man* in *The Spectator*.

11 (14 October; 11 November.) 'Education in a Changing World', five broadcasts printed in *The Listener*.

1932

12 CULTURE AND ANARCHY. BY MATTHEW ARNOLD. Edited with an introduction by JDW. Cambridge: at the University Press. [Paperback ed. 1960.]

13 *The Social and Political Ideas of some Representative Thinkers of the Victorian Age*. A series of lectures delivered at King's College, University of London, during the session 1931–2. Edited by F. J. C. Hearnshaw. [JDW's contribution was a lecture on 'Matthew Arnold and the Educationists'.]

1935

14 *Education of To-day*. A series of addresses delivered at the third Young Public School Masters' Conference at Harrow School in January 1935. Edited by E. D. Laborde. [JDW's address was entitled 'The Writing of English at School and Elsewhere'.]

1937

15 *The Life of Winifred Mercier*. By Lynda Grier. [Contains an introduction by JDW.]

III

EARLY WORKS (BIBLIOGRAPHICAL AND OTHER) ON ENGLISH LITERATURE AND PURITANISM

1905

16 JOHN LYLY. Cambridge: Macmillan and Bowes. Printed by John Clay at the University Press [reviewed by A. Feuillerat in *MLR*, 1].

1907

17 'A date in the Marprelate Controversy.' *The Library* (2nd ser.), VIII, 337–59.

1908

18 'The Missing Title of Thomas Lodge's Reply to Gosson's *School of Abuse*.' *MLR*, III, 166–8.

1909

19 (4 February.) 'The Legend of Sir Veritas.' *The New Age*, n.s. IV, 202. [A Spenserian skit *à propos* of a lengthy discussion on the subject of Miracles in *The New Age*, Chesterton, Belloc, Shaw, and Belford Bax being the chief disputants.]

20 (Spring.) *The Cambridge History of English Literature*. Vol. III. Renascence and Reformation. [Contains 'The Marprelate Controversy' by JDW.]

21 (April.) Review of William Pierce's *An Historical Introduction to the Marprelate Tracts*. *The Library* (2nd ser.), X, 214--18.

22 (July.) 'A new tract from the Marprelate press' [*An exhortation vnto the gouernours, and people of...Wales* 1588]. *Ibid.* X, 225–40.

23 (July.) 'Anthony Munday, Pamphleteer and Pursuivant.' *MLR*, IV, 484–90.

24 (29 July.) 'The Marprelate Controversy.' Letter to the *TLS* [a reply to the *TLS* review of *CHEL*, III].

25 (October.) 'The Rev. W. H. Hutton and *The Cambridge History of English Literature* [misprinted *Cambridge Modern*

History].' [A letter in *The Church Family Newspaper*, replying to Hutton's review.]

26 (October.) 'Euphues and the Prodigal Son.' *The Library* (2nd ser.), X, 337–61.

1910

27 *The Cambridge History of English Literature*. Vol. VI. The Drama to 1642 part II. [Contains 'The Puritan Attack upon the Stage' by JDW.]

28 THE WOUNDS OF CIVIL WAR. BY THOMAS LODGE (1594). [A Malone Society Reprint.]

29 (October.) 'Giles Fletcher and *The Faerie Queene*.' *MLR*, V, 493–4.

30 (October.) 'John Lyly's Relations by Marriage.' *Ibid.* V, 495–7.

1911

31 LIFE IN SHAKESPEARE'S ENGLAND. A BOOK OF ELIZABETHAN PROSE compiled by JDW. Cambridge: at the University Press. 2nd ed., 1913; Penguin ed., 1944. [See also no. 147 below.]

32 Review of A. Feuillerat's *John Lyly: Contribution à l'Histoire de la Renaissance en Angleterre*. *MLR*, VI, 103–14.

33 'Richard Schilders and the English Puritans.' *Transactions of the Bibliographical Society*, XI, 65–134.

1912

34 THE RESURRECTION OF OUR LORD. [A Malone Society Reprint in which JDW collaborated with Bertram Dobell.]

35 'Martin Marprelate and Shakespeare's Fluellin. A new theory of the authorship of the Marprelate tracts' [the case for Sir Roger Williams's authorship]. *The Library* (3rd ser.), III, 113–51; 241–76. [Reprinted from *The Library* and published by Alexander Moring Ltd. 1912.]

1913

36 'Did Sir Roger Williams write the Marprelate tracts? A rejoinder' [to R. B. McKerrow and W. Pierce]. *Ibid.* IV, 92–104.

IV

WAR-TIME AND JUST AFTER

1914

37 Review of J. M. Robertson's *The Baconian Heresy: a Confutation. MLR*, IX, 527–9.

38 THE WAR AND DEMOCRACY. By R. W. Seton-Watson, JDW, Alfred E. Zimmern, and Arthur Greenwood. London: Macmillan & Co., Ltd. [Planned and edited by AEZ and JDW as a study-book for WEA classes. Translated into many European languages. JDW's contributions are chapters on 'The National Idea in Europe, 1789–1914', and 'Russia'.]

39 ['Russia and her Ideals.' See no. 3 above.]

1916

40 POETRY AND THE CHILD. Oxford: at the University Press. English Association Pamphlet, no. 34.

41 'Prospects in English Literature.' Four articles by 'Muezzin' in *The Athenæum*: I, 'Poetry and Shop-keeping' (February); II, 'Pessimism and Prophecy' (March); III, 'Looking Backwards' (May); IV, 'The Great Schism' (June).

42 (April.) 'The Parallel Plots in *Hamlet*: a Reply to Dr W. W. Greg.' *MLR*, XIII, 129–56.

43 [*Humanism in the Continuation School*, written early in 1918. See no. 4 above.]

44 'The Copy for *Hamlet*, 1603.' *The Library* (3rd ser.), IX, 153–85.

45 'The *Hamlet* Transcript, 1593.' *Ibid.* IX, 217–47. [44 and 45 were reprinted as a single pamphlet by Alexander Moring Ltd.]

46 (16 May; 25 July.) 'Hamlet's Solid Flesh.' Letters to the *TLS*.

47 (4 July.) 'Shakespeare's Versification and the Early Texts.' *Ibid.*

48 (July; August.) 'The play-scene in "Hamlet" restored. I. Lock and Key.' *The Athenæum*.

49 (September; November.) 'The play-scene in "Hamlet" restored. II. The Multiple Mouse-Trap, and how it works.' [48 and 49 together form the first draft of *What Happens in Hamlet*, ch. v.]

50 (14 November; 2 January 1919.) 'Hatching the Cock's Egg of Polonius.' Letters to the *TLS*.

51 (With A. W. Pollard) 'What follows if some of the good Quarto editions of Shakespeare's plays were printed from his autograph manuscripts.' *Transactions of the Bibliographical Society*, xv, 136–9. [Summary of paper read 16 December 1918.]

52 (9, 16 January; 13 March; 7, 14 August.) 'The "Stolne and surreptitious" Shakespearian Texts: Why some of Shakespeare's plays were pirated; How some of Shakespeare's plays were pirated; Henry V (1600); Merry Wives of Windsor (1602); Romeo and Juliet, 1597.' [Five articles, with A. W. Pollard, in the *TLS*.]

53 (8 May; 29 May.) 'Shakespeare's Hand in the Play of "Sir Thomas More".' Letters to the *TLS*.

54 (22 January.) 'Sidelights on Shakespeare.' Letter to the *TLS* [in defence of Dugdale Sykes].

55 (29 January; 19 February.) 'Early Touring Companies.' Letters to the *TLS* [in controversy with W. J. Lawrence].

56 (April.) 'Dramatic and Bibliographical Problems in *Hamlet*.' *MLR*, xv, 163–6 [a reply to W. W. Greg's article in *MLR*, xiv, October 1919].

57 (30 September.) 'Elizabethan Printing.' Letter to the *TLS* [in reply to Bayfield].

58 (October.) 'A Note on Elisions in *The Faerie Queene*.' *MLR*, xv, 409–14.

59 (October.) Review of J. M. Robertson's *The Problem of 'Hamlet'*; Elmer Edgar Stoll's *Hamlet: An Historical and Comparative Study*; and V. Østerberg's *Studier over Hamlet-Teksterne*, I: *ibid*. xv, 434–40.

V

EDITING SHAKESPEARE, AND OTHER WORK MAINLY ELIZABETHAN

1921

60 THE WORKS OF SHAKESPEARE. Edited by Sir Arthur Quiller-Couch and JDW. [Quiller-Couch retired from the edition on the completion of the comedies in 1931. The texts alone, with enlarged glossaries, began to be reissued in 1957 as 'The Cambridge Pocket Shakespeare'. The volumes are listed separately below.]

61 THE TEMPEST. Cambridge: at the University Press. [This, and each succeeding play up to *The Winter's Tale* (1931), was edited by Sir Arthur Quiller-Couch and JDW, with an account of its stage-history by Harold Child. HC continued to contribute until *II Henry IV* and his death (November 1945).]

62 THE TWO GENTLEMEN OF VERONA.

63 THE MERRY WIVES OF WINDSOR.

64 (7, 21 April.) 'Shakespeare: a standard text.' Letters to the *TLS* [in controversy with G. Bernard Shaw].

1922

65 MEASURE FOR MEASURE.

66 THE COMEDY OF ERRORS.

67 MUCH ADO ABOUT NOTHING.

68 LOVE'S LABOUR'S LOST. [2nd ed., revised throughout, 1961.]

69 *Two Elizabethan stage abridgements: the Battle of Alcazar and Orlando Furioso: An essay in critical bibliography*, by W. W. Greg, 1923. [Contains (pp. 361–4) speculations by JDW on *Orlando* and its congeners (*The Famous Victories* and *A Shrew*) communicated in a private letter.]

70 *Shakespeare's Hand in the Play of Sir Thomas More.* Papers by Alfred W. Pollard and others. Cambridge: at the University Press. [Contains 'Bibliographical Links between the Three Pages and the Good Quartos' by JDW.]

71 A MIDSUMMER NIGHT'S DREAM.

72 *Studies in the First Folio, written for the Shakespeare Association in celebration of the First Folio Tercentenary and read at meetings of the Association held at King's College, University of London, May–June 1923. With an Introduction by Sir Israel Gollancz*, 1924. [Contains 'The Task of Heminge and Condell': a paper read by JDW on 18 May 1923. An interesting volume as containing papers by both Sidney Lee and W. W. Greg.]

73 (28 August.) 'Love's Labour's Lost' [IV. iii. 333]. Letter to the *TLS*.

74 (25 September; 16 October.) 'Shakespearian Elisions in *Sir Thomas More*.' Letters to the *TLS*.

75 (December.) 'Scilens.' Letter in the *London Mercury*, XI, 187 [reply to Grethe Hjort, in November issue].

76 *Essays and Studies by Members of the English Association*, vol. x, 1924. [Contains 'Spellings and Misprints in the Second Quarto of *Hamlet*' by JDW.]

1925

77 Review of J. A. Fort's *The Two Dated Sonnets of Shakespeare*, and *The Sonnets of Shakespeare*, edited by T. G. Tucker: *RES*, I, 353–9.

1926

78 THE MERCHANT OF VENICE.

79 AS YOU LIKE IT.

80 (2 April.) 'The Teacher's World and Shakespeare.' Article in the *Teacher's World*.

81 Review of Rudolf Fischer's *Shakespeares Sonette*: *RES*, II, 350–4.

82 Review of *Studies in Shakespeare, Milton and Donne* (University of Michigan publications, Language and Literature, vol. I): *ibid.* II, 475–9.

1927

83 (6 January.) 'Marlowe and *As You Like It*.' Letter to the *TLS*.

84 Review of J. M. Robertson's *The Problems of the Shakespeare Sonnets*: *Monthly Criterion*, VI, 162–7.

85 (October.) 'Act- and Scene-Divisions in the Plays of Shakespeare: a Rejoinder to Sir Mark Hunter' [art. in July 1926]. *RES*, III, 385–97. [See W. W. G.'s art. in *RES*, IV, 152–8.]

86 THE POETRY OF THE AGE OF WORDS-
WORTH. AN ANTHOLOGY OF THE FIVE
MAJOR POETS. Selected with an introduction by
JDW. Cambridge: at the University Press.

1928

87 THE TAMING OF THE SHREW.

88 THE TEMPEST. BY WILLIAM SHAKE-
SPEARE. A FACSIMILE OF THE FIRST
FOLIO TEXT. With an Introduction by JDW.
London: Faber and Gwyer.

89 TWELFTH NIGHT. BY WILLIAM SHAKE-
SPEARE. A FACSIMILE OF THE FIRST
FOLIO TEXT. With an Introduction by JDW.
London: Faber and Gwyer.

90 CORIOLANUS. BY WILLIAM SHAKE-
SPEARE. A FACSIMILE OF THE FIRST
FOLIO TEXT. With an Introduction by JDW.
London: Faber and Gwyer.

91 MACBETH. BY WILLIAM SHAKESPEARE.
A FACSIMILE OF THE FIRST FOLIO TEXT.
With an Introduction by JDW. London: Faber and
Gwyer.

92 (18 October; 1 November.) 'The Text of *Hamlet* I. ii.
129.' Letters to the *TLS*.

93 '"They Sleepe All the Act."' *RES*, IV, 191–3.

94 Review of D. Nichol Smith's *Shakespeare in the Eighteenth
Century*: *The Library* (4th ser.), IX, 223.

1929

95 ALL'S WELL THAT ENDS WELL.

96 ANTONY AND CLEOPATRA. BY WILLIAM SHAKESPEARE. A FACSIMILE OF THE FIRST FOLIO TEXT. With an Introduction by JDW. London: Faber and Gwyer.

97 THE WINTER'S TALE. BY WILLIAM SHAKESPEARE. A FACSIMILE OF THE FIRST FOLIO TEXT. With an Introduction by JDW. London: Faber and Gwyer.

98 AS YOU LIKE IT. BY WILLIAM SHAKESPEARE. A FACSIMILE OF THE FIRST FOLIO TEXT. With an Introduction by JDW. London: Faber and Gwyer.

99 JULIUS CAESAR. BY WILLIAM SHAKESPEARE. A FACSIMILE OF THE FIRST FOLIO TEXT. With an Introduction by JDW. London: Faber and Gwyer.

100 SIX TRAGEDIES OF SHAKESPEARE: AN INTRODUCTION FOR THE PLAIN MAN. London: Longmans, Green and Co.

101 OF GHOSTES AND SPIRITES WALKING BY NYGHT. BY LEWES LAVATER (1572). Edited with introduction and appendix by JDW and May Yardley. London: Oxford University Press for the Shakespeare Association.

102 *Proceedings of the British Academy 1929.* Vol. xv. [Contains 'The Elizabethan Shakespeare' by JDW: the Annual Shakespeare Lecture.]

103 (3 October.) 'Shakespeare's Puns on "Bonds"' [*Twelfth Night*, III. i. 24]. Letter to the *TLS*.

104 Review of *The Tragedie of Coriolanus*, edited by Horace Howard Furness, Jr.: *RES*, v, 215–18.

105 Review of G. F. Bradby's *The Problems of Hamlet*: *MLR*, xxiv, 373–4.

1930

106 TWELFTH NIGHT. [2nd ed., 1949.]

107 THE TRAGEDIE OF HAMLET PRINCE OF DENMARKE. BY WILLIAM SHAKE-SPEARE. Edited by JDW from the text of the second quarto. Illustrated by eighty wood engravings designed and cut by Edward Gordon Craig. And printed by Count Harry Kessler at the Cranach Press, Weimar. [A sequel to the Cranach *Hamlet* of 1929, the text of which is a German adaptation by Hauptmann. The 1930 volume contains the same cuts by Craig, but prints as consecutive borders to Shakespeare's text the stories by Saxo Grammaticus and Belleforest each accompanied by an English translation, while the whole concludes with an essay on 'The Text of *Hamlet*' and (in a jacket at the end) textual notes by JDW.]

108 'The Schoolmaster in Shakespeare's Plays.' *Essays by Divers Hands. Being the Transactions of the Royal Society of Literature*, n.s. ix, 9–34.

109 (17 April.) '"Sound" or "South"' [*Twelfth Night*, I. i. 5]. Letter to the *TLS*.

110 (19 June.) 'Textual Points in *As You Like It* and *Twelfth Night*.' Letter to the *TLS*.

111 Review of *Much Ado About Nothing*, Parallel Passage Edition, edited by Alphonso Gerald Newcomer, completed by Henry David Gray: *MLR*, xxv, 203–6.

112 'Thirteen Volumes of Shakespeare: a Retrospect.' *Ibid.* xxv, 397–414.

113 Review of Thomas Middleton's *A Game of* [*sic* for *at*] *Chesse*, edited by R. C. Bald: *The Library* (4th ser.), XI, 105–16.

1931

114 THE WINTER'S TALE.

115 HENRY V. BY WILLIAM SHAKESPEARE. A FACSIMILE OF THE FIRST FOLIO TEXT. With an Introduction by JDW. London: Faber and Faber.

116 KING LEAR. BY WILLIAM SHAKESPEARE. A FACSIMILE OF THE FIRST FOLIO TEXT. With an Introduction by JDW. London: Faber and Faber.

117 FIRST STEPS IN SHAKESPEARE. [Scenes from *A Midsummer Night's Dream*, *The Merchant of Venice*, *Julius Caesar*, *Macbeth*. Each issued separately.] Arranged and edited by JDW. Cambridge: at the University Press.

118 (April.) Review of E. K. Chambers's *William Shakespeare: a Study of Facts and Problems*: *MLR*, XXVI, 189–98.

119 (23 May.) 'Sir Philip Sidney', by Mona Wilson. Review in *The Spectator*.

120 (24 September; 29 October.) '*Hamlet*: a suggestion' [punctuation of *Hamlet*, II. ii. 307–14]. Letters to the *TLS*.

1932

121 THE ESSENTIAL SHAKESPEARE: A BIOGRAPHICAL ADVENTURE. Cambridge: at the University Press. [German trans., by Fromziska Meister, 1953; Serbo-Croat trans., 1960; Paperback ed., 1960.]

1933

122 PARADOXES OF DEFENCE. BY GEORGE SILVER (1599). A Shakespeare Association Facsimile, with an introduction by JDW.

123 (8 June; 31 August.) 'Shakespeare Emendations.' Letters to the *TLS*.

124 (6, 20 July.) 'The Nook-shotten isle of Albion' [*Henry V*, III. v. 14]. Letters to the *TLS*.

1934

125 HAMLET. [2nd ed., 1936; with 20 pages of 'Corrections and additional notes'.]

126 THE MANUSCRIPT OF SHAKESPEARE'S *HAMLET* AND THE PROBLEMS OF ITS TRANSMISSION. 2 vols. Cambridge: at the University Press. [An expansion of lectures delivered as Sandars Reader in Bibliography, 1932.]

127 (18 January.) 'The Duel in *Hamlet*.' Letter to the *TLS*.

128 (20 September.) 'The Manuscript of *Hamlet*.' Letter to the *TLS*.

1935

129 WHAT HAPPENS IN *HAMLET*. Cambridge: at the University Press. [The second edition (1937) contains a new preface and seven pages of notes. The third edition (1951) contains a new preface and a reprint (Appendix F) of a review of S. de Madariaga's *On Hamlet* (no. 178 below). Paperback ed., 1960.]

130 *The Great Tudors*, edited by Katharine Garvin. [Contains a chapter on 'William Shakespeare' by A. W. Pollard and JDW. Readers, if any, are challenged to disintegrate authorship. Reprinted 1956.]

131 (3, 24 January.) 'Too too sullied flesh.' Letters to the *TLS*.

132 (16, 30 May; 13 June.) '"The Genuine Text"' [the case for the entire *Hamlet*]. Letters to the *TLS*.

133 Review of Frances A. Yates's *John Florio, the life of an Italian in Shakespeare's England*: *MLR*, XXX, 522–4.

1936

134 KING JOHN.

135 THE MEANING OF *THE TEMPEST*. Newcastle upon Tyne: The Literary and Philosophical Society. The Robert Spence Watson Memorial Lecture, 1936.

136 (11, 25 January.) 'Was King Claudius a Usurper?' Letters to the *TLS*.

137 (14 April.) 'Shakespeare.' By Middleton Murry. Review in the *Manchester Guardian*.

138 (26 September; 17 October.) 'Prince Fortinbras.' Letters to the *TLS*.

139 (24 October; 7 November.) 'Perttaunt' [*Love's Labour's Lost*, v. ii. 67]. Letters to the *TLS*.

140 'The Study of Shakespeare.' *University of Edinburgh Journal*, VIII, 3–13. [Inaugural Lecture.]

1937

141 (16 January.) 'Shakespeare, Milton, and Congreve' [descriptions of Cleopatra, Dalila, and Millamant]. Letter to the *TLS*.

142 (17 March.) 'Shakespeare: the Scholar's Contribution'; a broadcast printed in *The Listener*.

1938

143 *Seventeenth Century Studies Presented to Sir Herbert Grierson*. [Contains a preface by JDW.]

144 (7 May.) '*Love's Labour's Lost*' [II. i. 222]. Letter to the *TLS*.

1939

145 RICHARD II.

146 LESLIE STEPHEN AND MATTHEW ARNOLD AS CRITICS OF WORDSWORTH. Cambridge: at the University Press. The Leslie Stephen Lecture, 1939.

147 THROUGH ELIZABETHAN EYES. An Abridgement of *Life in Shakespeare's England* for Junior Readers. [Contains a short preface and a glossary by JDW.]

148 'The Political Background of Shakespeare's *Richard II* and *Henry IV*. A Lecture delivered before the German Shakespeare Society at Weimar': *Shakespeare-Jahrbuch*, LXXV, 36–51.

1940

149 *The Cambridge Bibliography of English Literature*. [Articles in vol. I on 'The Puritan Attack upon the Stage' and 'The Marprelate Controversy' are by JDW with the help, respectively, of E. N. S. Thompson and A. F. S. Pearson.]

1942

150 Paraphrase of 'Nashe's "Kid in Æsop": a Danish Interpretation by V. Østerberg'. *RES*, XVIII, 385–94.

151 'Shakespeare's Universe.' *University of Edinburgh Journal*, XI, 216–33.

1943

152 THE FORTUNES OF FALSTAFF. Cambridge: at the University Press. The Clark Lectures, 1942–3.

153 (5 June.) 'Treasure in an old Book.' *Edinburgh Evening News*. [An account of the 'Shakespeare signature' discovered by the librarian of the Folger Memorial Library, Washington, in a copy of William Lambarde's Ἀρχαιονομία, *sive de priscis anglorum legibus libri*, 1568.]

1944

154 Review of Oliffe Richmond's *Challenge to Faith*: *University of Edinburgh Journal*, XIII, 134–6.

1945

155 (14 June.) Review of *Political Characters of Shakespeare*, by John Palmer, in *The Listener*.

156 (July.) Review of *Political Characters of Shakespeare*, by John Palmer, in *Britain To-day*.

157 'The Origins and Development of Shakespeare's *Henry IV.*' *The Library* (4th ser.), XXVI, 2–16.

1946

158 I HENRY IV.

159 II HENRY IV.

160 'A note on the Porter in "Macbeth".' *Edinburgh Bibliographical Society Transactions*, II, 413–16.

161 HENRY V. [The stage-history of this and of all succeeding plays was written by C. B. Young.]

162 MACBETH.

163 *Shakespeare on the Soviet Stage.* By Mikhail M. Morozov. Translated by David Magarshack. With an introduction by JDW.

164 Review of Peter Alexander's *Shakespeare's Punctuation*: *RES*, xxiii, 70–8.

165 (With R. W. Hunt) 'The Authenticity of Simon Forman's *Bocke of Plaies.*' *Ibid.* xxiii, 193–200 [193–7 by JDW].

166 (26 July.) 'Twelfth Night.' Letter to the *TLS*. [On Feste's song.]

167 'New Ideas and Discoveries about Shakespeare.' *The Virginia Quarterly Review*, xxiii, 537–42.

168 'The Joy of Editing Shakespeare', a ten-minute talk by JDW printed in *The Listener*, 27 November [not JDW's title!]. Followed by a long discussion with William Bliss (letters on 4, 11, 18, 25 December, 1, 8 January, 5, 12 February) on the character of the First Folio.

1948

169 TITUS ANDRONICUS.

170 Tribute to Walter de la Mare on his Seventy-fifth Birthday [25 April 1948]. Contains 'Variations on the theme of *A Midsummer Night's Dream*' by JDW [an elaboration of de la Mare's essay in disintegration, the introduction to his edition of *A Midsummer Night's Dream* (The Scholar's Library, Macmillan), 1935, reprinted in his *Pleasures and Speculations*, 1940].

171 *Shakespeare Survey 1*. [Contains '*Titus Andronicus* on the Stage in 1595', by JDW.]

1949

172 JULIUS CAESAR.

173 *Shakespeare Survey 2*. [Contains 'Ben Jonson and *Julius Caesar*', by JDW.]

174 POEMS | Printed by several Hands. | OXFORD | AT THE BODLEIAN LIBRARY | OVER AGAINST *THE KINGS ARMS* | 1949. [Contains a sonnet by Drayton first set up by JDW and later distributed and reset by F. P. Wilson.]

175 (24 June.) 'Titus Andronicus.' Letter to the *TLS*. [On Peacham illustration.]

176 (18 August.) 'The Text of the Plays', a broadcast printed in *The Listener*.

177 (30 September.) 'Rebellious Dead.' Letter to the *TLS*. [On *Macbeth*, IV. i. 97.]

178 Review of Salvador de Madariaga's *On Hamlet*: *MLR*, XLIV, 390–7.

1950

179 ANTONY AND CLEOPATRA.

180 (17 February.) 'The Wooing of Nerissa.' Letter to the *TLS*. [*Merchant of Venice*, III. ii. 199.]

181 (10 March.) 'Text Corruptions.' Letter to the *TLS*. [Reply to C. S. Lewis, 3 March, on verse 'fossils'.]

1951

182 *Shakespeare Survey 4*. [Contains 'Malone and the Upstart Crow', by JDW.]

183 *The Development of Shakespeare's Imagery*. By W. H. Clemen, with a preface by JDW.

184 (29 June.) 'The Upstart Crow.' Letter to the *TLS*. [Reply to Janet Spens.]

185 '*Titus and Vespasian* and Professor Alexander.' *MLR*, XLVI, 250.

1952

186 I HENRY VI.

187 II HENRY VI.

188 III HENRY VI.

189 SHAKESPEARE'S HISTORIES AT STRATFORD 1951. By JDW and T. C. Worsley. London: Max Reinhardt. JDW contributed 'Shakespeare and English History as the Elizabethans understood it'.

190 Review of *Macbeth*, edited by Kenneth Muir: *RES*, n.s. III, 71–5.

191 Review of H. N. Paul's *The Royal Play of Macbeth: When, why, and how it was written by Shakespeare*: ibid. n.s. III, 386–8.

192 'Shakespeare's *Richard III* and *The True Tragedy of Richard the Third*, 1594.' *Shakespeare Quarterly*, III, 299–306.

193 Rejoinder to R. Flatter's review of *Macbeth*: *Modern Philology*, XLIX, 274–5.

1954

194 RICHARD III.

195 *Talking of Shakespeare*. Edited by John Garrett. [A selection of twelve lectures from the annual courses for teachers delivered at Stratford between 1948 and 1953. JDW's is entitled 'On editing Shakespeare, with special reference to the problems of *Richard III*'.]

196 *Shakespeare Survey 7*. [Contains 'The New Way with Shakespeare's Texts: An Introduction for Lay Readers. I. The Foundations', by JDW.]

1955

197 (With G. I. Duthie) ROMEO AND JULIET.

198 *Shakespeare Survey 8*. [Contains 'The New Way with Shakespeare's Texts: An Introduction for Lay Readers. II. Recent work on the text of *Romeo and Juliet*', by JDW.]

199 Review of D. Hay's *Polydore Vergil: Renaissance Historian, and man of letters*: *MLR*, L, 66–8.

1956

200 PERICLES. [Edited by J. C. Maxwell, with a prefatory note by JDW.]

201 *Shakespeare Survey 9*. [Contains 'The New Way with Shakespeare's Texts: An Introduction for Lay Readers. III. In sight of Shakespeare's Manuscripts', by JDW.]

202 Review of Percy Simpson's *Studies in Elizabethan Drama*: *RES*, n.s. VII, 423–4.

1957

203 (With Alice Walker) OTHELLO.

204 TROILUS AND CRESSIDA. [Edited by Alice Walker, with a prefatory note by JDW.]

205 TIMON OF ATHENS. [Edited by J. C. Maxwell, with a prefatory note by JDW.]

206 *Shakespeare Survey 10*. [Contains 'Shakespeare's "small Latin"—how much?' by JDW.]

207 (2 September.) 'The Shakespeare Paradox'. *The Times*.

208 Review of *Essays by Divers Hands, being the Transactions of the Royal Society of Literature*, New Series, vol. XXVII, edited by Sir George Rostrevor Hamilton: *RES*, n.s. VIII, 336–9.

209 (October.) 'A Note on *Richard III*: the Bishop of Ely's Strawberries.' *MLR*, LII, 563–4.

1958

210 *Shakespeare Survey 11*. [Contains 'The New Way with Shakespeare's Texts: An Introduction for Lay Readers. IV. Towards the High Road', by JDW.]

211 'The Composition of the Clarence Scenes in *Richard III*.' *MLR*, LIII, 211–14.

212 Brief introductions to *Hamlet, King Lear, Othello,* and *Macbeth* written for the British Council to be translated in various languages and dialects of India, mainly for women readers.

1960

213 CYMBELINE. [Edited by J. C. Maxwell, with a prefatory note by JDW.]

214 (With G. I. Duthie) KING LEAR.

215 *The Living Shakespeare*. Edited by Robert Gittings. London: Heinemann. [Contains 'The Texts' by JDW. 'Closely based' on a series of broadcasts for the B.B.C.]

1961

216 CORIOLANUS.

217 (25 May) 'The Works of William Shakespeare... recorded by Argo for the Marlowe Society', in *The Guardian*.

VI

PERSONALIA

1944

218 *Proceedings of the British Academy 1944.* Vol. xxx. [Contains 'George Charles Moore Smith', by JDW: an obituary.]

1945

219 *Proceedings of the British Academy 1945.* Vol. xxxi. [Contains 'Alfred William Pollard', by JDW: an obituary.]

1956

220 *Proceedings of the British Academy 1956.* Vol. xlii. [Contains an obituary of Sir Edmund Chambers by F. P. Wilson, to which JDW contributed.]

1959

221 *Elizabethan and Jacobean Studies Presented to Frank Percy Wilson in Honour of his Seventieth Birthday.* [Contains 'Memories of Harley Granville-Barker and Two of his Friends', by JDW.]

222 Part of 'Walter Wilson Greg, 9 July 1875–4 March 1959'. *The Library* (5th ser.), xiv, 151–74. [JDW's contribution, pp. 153–7.]

223 'The Presentation of Finnish Runos', by T. J. Mustanoja. *Neuphilologische Mitteilungen*, lx, 1–11. [Contains (pp. 9–10) a memory by JDW of runo-singing by two Finnish bards, 1907.]

www.ingramcontent.com/pod-product-compliance
Ingram Content Group UK Ltd.
Pitfield, Milton Keynes, MK11 3LW, UK
UKHW042149280225
455719UK00001B/220